LOVING GOD WITH ALL MY HEART

God . . . wants your whole heart,
even if it comes to Him in broken, jagged pieces.
SUSAN LENZKES

Julie Ackerman Link

Loving God with All My Heart

© 2004 Julie Ackerman Link

Discovery House Publishers is affiliated with RBC Ministries,
Grand Rapids, Michigan 49501.

Requests for permission to quote from this book should be directed to:
Permissions Department, Discovery House Publishers, P.O. Box 3566,
Grand Rapids, MI 49501.

Scripture quotations are taken from the Holy Bible, New International
Version®. © 1973, 1978, 1984 by International Bible Society. Used by
permission of Zondervan Publishing House. All rights reserved.

Cover Photos: PictureQuest (background, olive tree)
                 Dean Ohlman (inset, olives)

Printed in the United States of America
04 05 06 07 08 09 10 / EB / 10 9 8 7 6 5 4 3 2 1

Introduction

Standing on the eastern side of the Jordan River, not far from where Moses stood to view the Promised Land, I gazed across the Jordan Valley and tried to imagine standing alongside the ancient Israelites, seeing for the first time the land that God referred to as "flowing with milk and honey."

"Did this look a lot different when the Israelites got here?" I asked our guide.

I didn't want my disappointment to show, but I was expecting something dramatic, a stunning view that would make me gasp at its beauty and its startling contrast to the wilderness landscape on the eastern side of the Jordan.

"No," she answered. "This is how it has looked for thousands of years."

I searched my mental archives for an explanation that would reconcile what I was expecting with what I was seeing. The other side of the Jordan looked much the same as where I was standing.

Later I asked the question in a different way. "What do you think the Israelites saw when they got here?"

Our guide quickly answered, "The biggest oasis on the face of the whole earth," referring to what is now the city of Jericho.

I realized then why I couldn't see the Promised Land as the Israelites had. I had not spent forty years trekking around a hot, dusty desert. I had ridden across the barren landscape in the luxury of an air-conditioned tourist bus stocked with cold bottled water. To me, an oasis was nothing spectacular. To the Israelites, the sprawling patch of pale green they could see in the hazy distance indicated the presence of water—an abundant supply of life-sustaining water.

To see the beauty of the Promised Land requires a change in perspective. It has to be viewed through the eyes of one who is thirsty and who recognizes it as the place chosen by God to raise His family and nurture them in truth and trust.

Before visiting Israel, I pictured the Holy Land as drab and dust-covered. Childhood Bible lessons in fuzzy flannelgraph left the impression that the color palette of Bible lands ranged from olive green to desert brown.

But after spending time in Israel, I see it differently. In fact, every picture I now see is beautiful. For what makes Israel lovely is not the predominance of brilliant colors, but finding spots of color in so many unexpected places.

The psalmist wrote, "Taste and see that the LORD is

good." The milk and honey of God's goodness are often found in unexpected places, sometimes even dry, difficult places, but once we experience it, we'll long for more of it, and we'll lose our desire for all lesser substitutes.

Eat what you want and lose weight. Promises like this clutter the covers of women's magazines month after month. And women *want* to believe them. We want to believe that there is an easy, painless way to have the perfect body. Give us a plan, and we will eagerly follow it—at least for a day or two, maybe even a week.

But if these diets work so well, why do we need a new one every month in every magazine? And why do so many of us continue our battle of the bulge year after year?

The truth is, the only way to eat what we want and lose weight is to *want* what causes weight loss. In other words, desires have to change before diets will work. The desire to be thin is not enough; we must also desire what will make us thin—nutritious foods and plenty of exercise.

This is not information that anyone wants to hear. We

7

don't *want* to change our desires; we want our desires satisfied!

Health officials have estimated that more than 60 percent of Americans are overweight, and a Google search for "weight loss" turned up 5.7 million results.

Starvation is not our problem.

Hunger, however, is.

We are hungry for something, but it's not food. Even when we stuff our stomachs, we remain emotionally starved.

The desire to feel satisfied has led us to believe that feeling hunger is bad, so we look for eating programs that guarantee weight loss without nagging hunger pangs or rude growling sounds.

Hunger, however, is an ally, not an enemy. Hunger keeps us alive. God created it for a purpose and uses it for our good, both physically and spiritually:

He humbled you, causing you to hunger and then feeding you with manna, which neither you nor your fathers had known, to teach you that man does not live on bread alone but on every word that comes from the mouth of the LORD. (Deuteronomy 8:3)

Hunger is meant to remind us of our need for God, and having hunger satisfied is meant to remind us to be grateful: "When you have eaten and are satisfied, praise the LORD your God for the good land he has given you" (Deuteronomy 8:10). But in the twisted economy of sin, food is thought of as something we deserve—a reward for good

> The true mortification of our carnal nature is not a simple matter of denial and discipline. It is an internal, spiritual matter of finding more contentment in Christ than in food.
>
> **JOHN PIPER**

behavior or hard work—rather than an indication of God's love and care for creation.

God also designed hunger to motivate us to keep working: "The laborer's appetite works for him; his hunger drives him on" (Proverbs 16:26).

Jesus raised the subject of hunger to a new level in His Sermon on the Mount. He used it as a metaphor to explain that it is good to hunger and thirst for righteousness, for those who do "will be filled" (Matthew 5:6).

Sadly, however, righteousness seldom makes it to the top of our "most wanted" list, which, of course, is why we so seldom feel as if we are filled.

The desire to eat when we're hungry is good because food sustains life. The desire to eat when we're not hungry is bad because food then replaces life.

"Food is killing us in so many ways," said Amy

Wilensky, author of *The Weight of It,* in an interview on the Diane Rehm radio program. Using food as the method of choice, women are committing slow suicide with one of two extremes. By either stuffing or starving ourselves, we use the good that God gives to sustain life in ways that actually take our lives instead. What God intended to make us strong makes us weak when used inappropriately —too much, too little, too sweet, too fat. Each of these springs from desire gone awry. What God meant for good, we use for harm.

Man finds it hard to get what he wants, because he does not want the best; God finds it hard to give, because He would give the best, and man will not take it.

GEORGE MACDONALD

Popular media perpetuate the mistaken notion that being thin will make us desirable, and that by becoming desirable we'll be truly loved. Failing to identify the lie, many Christians join others who are using food and exercise to achieve not only physical perfection but also emotional satisfaction.

But it doesn't work. Our desires lead us astray.

Faulty Solutions Cause More Problems

Food, of course, is just one example of the many things we use inappropriately to eliminate uncomfortable feelings. The solutions we choose may differ, but the problem we're trying to solve is the same: emotional hunger. And when we try to satisfy emotional needs in physical ways we end up feeling bad about ourselves.

A friend of mine quotes a marketing expert who claims that people are motivated by two basic desires: to gain pleasure and to avoid pain.

Judging from the spam in my e-mail box, I'd say that

the message is getting through. The products most frequently promoted involve one of the two—usually in the form of pills to enhance sexual pleasure or to eliminate physical or psychological pain. (The next time you're curious as to why competing drug stores are located on three corners of so many intersections, stop and think about what they are really selling.)

There is only one big thing—desire. And before it, when it is big, all is little.

WILLA CATHER

If we are in physical or emotional pain, we want relief, and we want it fast. If we are not in pain, we want pleasure, and we want it without consequence or obligation.

Desire is not known for its patience, generosity, or commitment to excellence. When we want something— whether pleasure or relief—we want it in a way that is fast, easy, and inexpensive. We'd rather try every empty promise than admit that we need to change our desire. Desire does not want to be told that it can be satisfied only by changing. Desire wants satisfaction, not a morality lesson.

The idea that we have to *want* what is good for us goes against everything desire tells us.

The mistaken notion that every desire deserves to be satisfied is dangerous in the physical and emotional realm, but even more dangerous when carried over into our spiritual lives because it infects our interpretation of Scripture and our understanding of God.

Passages like Psalm 37:4 are particularly vulnerable to this kind of sabotage. "Delight yourself in the LORD and he will give you the desires of your heart" sounds to me like an invitation to order every book on my Amazon.com wish list. Upon closer scrutiny, however, I see that the verse has an introductory phrase that makes the meaning quite different. The promise only "works" when I desire the delight of the Lord. When people misread and misuse this verse they end up blaming God for failing to keep a promise He never made.

Although I know this is true, many of my prayers still sound like this: "Lord, I delight in you. Now can I have what I want? I'd like to be healthy, ageless, and thin. That's not too much to ask, is it?"

The War of Wants

Our desires are at war within us. Not only do we want to enjoy the taste of food, we want to eat as much as we want of whatever we want. Not only do we want to feel the satisfaction of a full stomach, we want never to feel hunger and never to be fat. Not only do we want to maintain a

Of all the fads which have affected mankind, none seems more difficult to explain than the desire of American women for the barberpole figure.

DR. MORRIS FISHBEIN

healthy weight, we want to be thin enough to fit into size eight (or less) jeans.

Clearly, our desires are in disarray. But this is not news. Since Eve's encounter with the serpent in Eden, we all have had to struggle with desires gone awry.

I want all kinds of things that aren't necessarily bad but which get in the way of things that are much better, and which often entice me to use ways of getting them that are bad for others as well as myself.

I desire . . .

to be well thought of (so I say flattering things to people I do not think well of).

to be beautiful (so I buy clothes, makeup, and other products to hide my imperfections).

to be smart (so I buy books I don't have time to read).

to be organized (so I buy notebooks, gadgets, and filing
  systems that just give me more places to lose things).

to be right (so I learn to use words in convincing ways).

When our desires compete with God's desires, conflict
and chaos invade our lives like a swarm of angry bees:

> What causes fights and quarrels among you?
> Don't they come from your desires that
> battle within you? You want something but
> don't get it. You kill and covet, but you
> cannot have what you want. You quarrel and
> fight. You do not have, because you do not
> ask God. When you ask, you do not receive,
> because you ask with wrong motives, that
> you may spend what you get on your
> pleasures. (James 4:1–3)

In a Bible study based on the ideas I've been exploring to write this book, the women in my group were answering the question "What (or who) is your biggest frustration?" Surprisingly, we all gave pretty much the same answer: ourselves. For one it was her impatience with her children; for another it was her inability to lose weight; for another it was her inability to say no to speaking invitations; for another it was her propensity to disappoint her parents.

Frankly, I was surprised by the responses because I expected to be the only one whose biggest enemy is myself. My biggest frustration is my inability to bring order to my life. This problem manifested itself during childhood but didn't become debilitating until I went off to college and no longer had my parents maintaining structure for me.

The problem went from being an annoying weakness to a spiritual defect when a well-meaning retreat speaker (one who evidently does not struggle with this area of ineptitude) asked this probing question: "When people look inside your car or closet, do they see any evidence that you believe in a God who brings order out of chaos?"

I've hated that question since the moment I heard it. But I hate the answer even more because I've always had to admit that the answer is "no." If it were up to me, no one would have reason to conclude that I believe in, am acquainted with, or, much less, am made in the image of a God who brings order out of chaos.

Having to admit this has caused me much guilt and anxiety. The guilt comes from

When we recognize there is nothing more precious than closeness to God, then every character flaw is seen as an intruder trying to break up that relationship.

NOAH WEINBERG

the belief that God hates my disorderly ways. The anxiety comes from the fear that maybe He also hates me.

In trying to reconcile my fears and feelings with the truth I know about God, I've discovered two points of view.

Some people say that I just need to try harder. God wants me to be neat, so if I want it badly enough I will be. So I try binge cleaning. When I get everything in place I feel good about myself. But only for a while. Within hours the mess is back. Like Pigpen in the *Peanuts* comic strip, I am followed by a cloud of debris.

Others say that being messy is part of being creative and I should just accept myself. God made me this way, so I might as well stop trying to be neat. So I begin rationalizing that being messy is just an innocuous character trait, not an insidious defect. And I feel better about myself. But only for a while. I am soon reminded why being messy is not a good way to live—disorder makes life difficult!

So the tension mounts. If I follow the first advice, I'm in danger of becoming like the Pharisees, who led perfectly ordered lives but kept the filth of greed and wickedness in their hearts. If I follow the second advice, I'm in danger of becoming like the pagans, who led undisciplined lives because they failed to make any distinction between clean and unclean.

As I've struggled to reconcile these two extremes and come to terms with my inadequacy, I've been relieved to discover a third alternative. More important than keeping a clean car or closet is to have a clean heart. Jesus put it this way: "First clean the inside . . . and then the outside also will be clean" (Matthew 23:26).

The relevant question I need to ask then is not, "What

does the contents of my closet say to the world about God?" It's "What does the contents of my heart say to God about me?"

When the first question is more important than the second, I am in violation of the first commandment. For the thing that frustrates me the most is a reliable indicator of my highest desire, and my highest desire indicates what I worship. On most days, my highest desire is for order, not for God.

God's Top Ten List

The Bible doesn't give a reason as to why the Ten Commandments are given in the order they are, but it's interesting to note that the tenth commandment

> Desire is a restless activity, a yearning for something one craves but does not possess. Love, even though it is passionate, has within it an element of repose, of satisfaction, of joy that comes from delight in the presence of the beloved.
>
> ROBERT LOUIS WILKEN

22

correlates to the first sin—desire: You shall not *want* what isn't yours.

From an earthly standpoint (i.e., looking up from our perspective rather than down from God's), it makes sense to consider the Ten Commandments in reverse order, kind of like a David Letterman Top Ten List, giving first consideration to commandment number ten. After all, if we don't covet, we will pretty much eliminate all of our reasons to lie, steal, or commit adultery.

Even the popular psalm of David, known for its comfort in times of loss, gives prominence to the subject of covetousness by reminding us first of all that those who follow the Good Shepherd have no reason to covet: "The LORD is my shepherd, I shall not be in want" (Psalm 23:1), or, as the Jewish Bible translates it, "I lack nothing."

I don't always feel as if that is true, though. My

emotions keep telling me that God is withholding something good or trying to trick me into settling for something inferior.

Nevertheless, I know that I *ought* to want God's will. So I pray, "Lord, I want to want your will. I want to want what you desire. I know this falls short of where I ought to be, but is it anything you can work with?"

Thankfully it is, and He does.

God doesn't have an easy job being our shepherd. We are like daylight savings time: either springing ahead or falling behind. We covet both the past and the future and disregard the only time we have: today.

We stand on tiptoes trying to see where God is taking us instead of trusting Him to get us there. When we are in the shadow, we assume that we are under a thundercloud rather than in the shelter of God's wings. When we are in the sunlight, we worry that it won't last. When the wind of trouble starts to howl, we hold on so it can't blow us away rather than let go so it can lift us up.

The birds that nest in the bush outside my office window demonstrate more faith than I do. They do not covet any more time than God gives them. They follow God's rhythm and never miss a beat. They don't debate whether it's time to fly or rest. They don't try to repeat yesterday or change tomorrow. They accept each day as a gift and use it to do what needs to be done: find food, build nests, sing, mate, and teach their offspring to fly.

I wish it were easy to release the past and relinquish the future. I wish I could accept what comes from God's hand each day as a carefully chosen gift. When the gift is stillness, I wish I would wait in quiet contentment and trust that God will not leave me stranded, that the same Spirit

Who got me to a certain place will take me to the next place at God's proper time. When the gift is wind, I wish that I would catch it and soar.

Jesus said that we shouldn't borrow trouble from the past or the future because each day has enough of its own (Matthew 6:34), but my fear of losing what I have, or not getting what I want, keeps me hanging on to what I should release and never gaining what God wants me to have.

Wanting What God Wants

Loving God with all our heart means desiring God as He desires us; it means having the relationship with God that He desires to have with us.

Before heading to Gethsemane, Jesus prayed,

"Father, I desire that they also whom You gave Me may be with Me where I am, that they may behold My glory which You have given Me; for You loved Me before the foundation of the world." (John 17:24 NKJV)

But before we can love God so unreservedly, we need to trust that God wants what is good for us and be assured that God's highest desire is our highest good.

The apostle Paul assures us that God cares about our emotional well-being when he refers to Him as "the Father of compassion and the God of all comfort" (2 Corinthians 1:3–7). But God doesn't simply want to mitigate our suffering; He wants to infuse our lives with joy. In fact, enjoyment was built into His perfect plan for creation. God wants us to enjoy work, to enjoy others, and to enjoy Him.

GOD WANTS US TO ENJOY OUR WORK.

Work was part of creation *before* the fall. Work is a blessing, not a curse, and God's desire for each of us is to have meaningful work that matches our gifts and abilities and makes an important contribution to the world.

"When God gives any man wealth and possessions, and enables him to enjoy

them, to accept his lot and be happy

[M]y chosen ones will long enjoy the works of their hands.

Isaiah 65:22

in his work—this is a gift of God. (Ecclesiastes 5:19)

God also wants us to rest. Even

though work is good, it has an inherent danger. The results and rewards of work can make us feel as if our work is more important than God's. So God ordained a Sabbath day of rest to remind us that we are dependent on His work, not vice versa.

[A]nyone who enters God's rest also rests from his own work, just as God did from his.

Let us, therefore, make every effort to enter that rest, so that no one will fall by following their example of disobedience. (Hebrews 4:10–11)

Sadly, many have come to think of rest as just another restriction imposed by a demanding God rather than as a gift from a loving Father who knows and wants what is good for all His children.

GOD WANTS US TO ENJOY ONE ANOTHER.

God created Eve so that Adam would have a companion. Alone, we are incomplete. God knows that for us to live fully and completely, we need to be engaged in peaceful, harmonious relationships with others and with Him. Many times, however, due to such human weaknesses as selfishness and pride, we break the peace. So God's instructions include guidelines not only for maintaining peace but also for restoring peace.

1. *Be quick to listen, slow to speak, and slow to become angry,* for anger "does not bring about the righteous life that God desires" (James 1:20).

2. *Be forgiving.* "Bear with each other and forgive whatever grievances you may have against one another. Forgive as the Lord forgave you" (Colossians 3:13).

3. *Be imitators of God.* "[A]s dearly loved children . . . live a life of love, just as Christ loved us and gave himself up for us as a fragrant offering and sacrifice to God" (Ephesians 5:1–2).

4. *Be ministers of reconciliation.* "All this is from God, who reconciled us to himself through Christ and gave us the ministry of reconciliation: that God was reconciling the world to himself in Christ, not counting men's sins against

them. And he has committed to us the message of reconciliation" (2 Corinthians 5:18–19).

GOD WANTS US TO ENJOY HIM.

The Westminster Catechism states that the chief and highest end for all people "is to glorify God, and fully to enjoy him forever."

This goes against the thinking of those who believe that God is a spoil sport who wants to squelch everything that is fun by arbitrarily labeling it "sin." On the contrary, over and over in Scripture, God says things like this:

> [I]n the presence of the LORD your God,
> you and your families shall eat and shall
> rejoice in everything you have put your hand
> to, because the LORD your God has blessed
> you. (Deuteronomy 12:7)

The prophet Habakkuk wrote, "I will rejoice in the LORD, I will be joyful in God my Savior" (3:18).

Among the many ways we can enjoy God are these:

1. *In Seeking Him*. People sometimes grumble because God doesn't make His presence more obvious. They complain that God is too difficult to find, too distant.

However, anyone who can remember being a child knows the delight of finding something that has been hidden. So surely God knows that there is little excitement in finding something we've not had to look for. Even Jesus said that He came "to seek and to save what was lost" (Luke 19:10).

God could, of course, make His presence more evident if He wanted to. He did in fact do so among the ancient Israelites. But they complained about *that*. When God delivered the Ten Commandments, His presence was accompanied by thunder, lightning, and smoke. The people were so terrified that they said to Moses, "Speak to us yourself and we will listen. But do not have God speak to us or we will die" (Exodus 20:19). It seems as if God can't win. People accuse Him of being difficult to please, but a more accurate conclusion is that we are difficult to please.

2. *In Celebrating His Goodness.* God planned feasts and celebrations into the yearly calendar. There were seven major holidays, some lasting as long as a week, and three of them were to be celebrated in one giant gathering in Jerusalem. Like rest, worship was not a duty demanded by a needy god, but a delight planned by a loving and giving God.

3. *In Following His Commands.* God knows us so well that He can foresee the results of our behavior. He also knows that much of what we think will make us happy will bring misery instead, so He gives us guidance to help us avoid

the grief that results from bad choices. When we realize this, we will delight in God's commands.

"Praise the Lord. Blessed is the man who fears the Lord, who finds great delight in his commands" (Psalm 112:1).

Feeling What God Feels

When we truly want what God wants, we'll begin feeling what God feels. We will weep with those who weep and rejoice with those who rejoice, just as God does. We'll sorrow over sin and rejoice in righteousness. We'll be angry at every injustice and we'll be eager to dispense grace and forgiveness.

The suggestion that we should allow ourselves to feel what God feels is frightening to some people, especially to those who have been hurt by someone who claimed to love them. Some go to great lengths to avoid feeling anything because the only feeling they know is pain. And for some, pain begins so early in life that the only coping mechanism they ever learn is to run from it (often by escaping into bad relationships) or to become numb to it (usually with substances or habits that minimize all feeling).

Sandbox Stoicism

At five years of age I began to believe that people who are strong refuse to feel pain. It started when my uncle chose to take his own life. In addition to my aunt, he left behind three teenage daughters and a five-year-old son.

One of the laws of physics says that for every action there is an equal and opposite reaction. That was true of my uncle's single gunshot. His tragic choice changed the course of many lives, including my own.

My cousin Dan came to live with our family while my aunt put together the pieces of her life. Dan and I became best friends and worst enemies. We did everything together and we fought the whole time. Dan had a reason for being difficult, I now realize; he had lost his father forever. But I did not; I simply had to share my parents for a few months. Both of us, however, were *feeling* cheated, and so the competition began. He was the first to learn to ride a two-wheeler without training wheels. I was the first to learn to read.

Having separate areas of interest and expertise should have made a healthy, balanced relationship. But we weren't content to be equal; we each wanted to be superior.

The battle escalated until the day it reached a peak in our backyard sandbox. Dan and I were arguing, as usual, and my mother was trying to get us to stop, as usual. She warned us that a spanking was her next alternative, but neither of us was willing to let the other have the last word.

When our arguing reached a decibel level high enough to disrupt the neighborhood, we heard the screen door slam and we knew punishment was on its way. Mother marched out to the sandbox, pulled me to my feet, and spanked my rear. I took my punishment without a whimper. Dan got spanked next, but he too refused to shed a tear.

Our stubborn stoicism made Mom fear that we were on our way to becoming hardened juvenile delinquents. She warned us once more to stop fighting and then went back into the house.

Dan and I did stop arguing, but not because of the punishment we'd just endured. We stopped because the argument had become moot; it was no longer possible for either of us to win.

Years later Dan and I told my mother why we both remained stone-faced on that simmering summer day. The subject of our fight had been whether boys or girls were bigger crybabies.

Unfortunately, the pride I felt that day for my impressive display of emotional and physical stoicism did not develop into strong character; instead it grew into disdain for emotion and a stubborn refusal to display any.

Pain is part of every life, and it's human nature to believe that pain is punishment. It's also human nature to try to avoid it. But avoidance can carry a high price tag.

For many years I tried to keep a safe distance from God because I feared that if I made myself too noticeable He would punish me for my imperfections. To keep from getting hurt, I foolishly reasoned, I would keep my distance. Feeling nothing would be better than feeling bad.

It took many years before I realized that I could not be a complete person without acknowledging the emotional side of my being. The realization came when I started questioning why I could not feel any love for God, a feeling which other Christians seemed to experience and enjoy. The reason, I learned, was that I had spent so many years trying not to feel anything.

Choose to Feel

A bumper sticker on a blue van caught my attention as I drove downtown for lunch. "Choose to Feel" it read.

As I considered the phrase, I noticed the billboards I was passing. Many of them sent a different message, a message urging me to choose things that would keep me from feeling—alcohol to deaden emotional pain; fat-laden food to alleviate feelings of emptiness; luxury cars, diamonds, and other expensive items to lessen feelings of worthlessness.

I started thinking then about how many temptations lure us away from God by promising to relieve emotional hurt that is the consequence of sin—our own or someone else's.

But God set a different example. Rather than become numb or indifferent to the pain of sin, God feels all of it and even allows us to witness Him suffer the results of it. Through the prophet Hosea, God expressed His own heart-wrenching pain caused by the loss of a wayward child (Hosea 11).

When we choose to feel the full range of our emotions —even sadness—we come to a fuller understanding of the

God who created us in His image—the image of One who feels.

When we turn off our feelings, run from them, or anesthetize them with habits or substances, we rob God of the opportunity to do what He does so well—comfort us; and we rob ourselves of learning how to comfort others. God "comforts us in all our troubles, so that we can comfort those in any trouble with the comfort we ourselves have received from God. For just as the sufferings of Christ flow over into our lives, so also through Christ our comfort overflows" (2 Corinthians 1:4–5).

Despite well-meaning claims to the contrary, few people have the patience to listen very long to the erratic beating of a hurting heart. But that's what God wants to do for us, and that's what He wants us to do for others.

In an episode of *Law and Order,* the captain said to

Elliot, "Don't worry when you feel something; worry when you don't." I think Jesus would say the same thing.

Shortly after his death in 2003, country music legend Johnny Cash won a Grammy Award for his short video titled "Hurt." The first line of the lyric is "I hurt myself today, to see if I still feel," and the remainder of the video illustrates what we know but refuse to believe: What makes us feel good one moment can deaden our feelings the next, leaving pain as the only proof that we still can feel.

The Oil of Joy

Heart disease kills thousands of people every year, and pharmaceutical companies make billions of dollars selling drugs that prevent hardening of the arteries, one of the causes of life-threatening heart disease. In fact, the top-selling drug in the world is one that prevents cholesterol from depositing a plaque-like substance in arteries.

A more serious condition, however, receives little attention and can't be prevented by any wonder drug. It's called hardening of the heart, and the Bible warns against it. "[H]e who hardens his heart falls into trouble" (Proverbs 28:14).

A hard heart is one that refuses correction and thus keeps repeating the same mistakes. The Pharaoh of Egypt had this condition. Pain to him was an annoyance to get rid of, not a warning to heed. As soon as discomfort went away, he went back to his same stubborn ways.

Interestingly, a common Middle Eastern fruit is key to the prevention of both hardening of the arteries and hardening of the heart.

Several popular diets and many health experts

recommend the use of olive oil in place of other fats in our diet. Olive oil is high in good cholesterol and low in the bad kind. It softens arteries instead of hardening them. It's an apt symbol, therefore, for the plea made by the psalmist David: "Today, if you hear his voice, do not harden your hearts . . ." (Psalm 95:7–8).

According to today's values, the descendents of Ishmael got the good oil—black gold; whereas the descendents of Isaac got only black olives.

Adding olive oil to our diets won't prevent the spiritual condition known as hardening of the heart, of course. But whenever we use it in our food we can also use it as a reminder to check the condition of our hearts for symptoms of spiritual hardness such as stubbornness, impatience, bad temper, indifference, greed.

Today we think of olive oil as something found in

44

decorative bottles and used for cooking. But in biblical times it served so many purposes that it came to be known as a symbol of joy. Olive oil was not only food but also fuel. It was used to anoint kings and heal the sick. It brought pleasure by seasoning food, soothing dryness, creating warmth, and illuminating darkness.

In addition, olives have long been used as a symbol of peace, which is God's highest desire for His people. Peace with God—shalom—is a world the way it ought to be—a world restored to God's original intention—a world filled with worshipers adoring the One who created them, sustains them, and longs to lavish them with all that is good and pleasing and beautiful.

From Eden to Gethsemane

From the first to the final garden, the plot of Scripture

revolves around desire. In the first garden, desire was perverted; in the last garden it was purified.

Desire determined what Eve did—she *wanted* food that was pleasing, so she followed bad advice, and evil slithered into creation.

Desire determined what Jesus did—He *wanted* to please God so He gave up His own life for ours, and innocence returned to creation.

Desire determines what God does—He *wants* us to know that He loves us so He does everything He can to convince us that He desires our good by supplying us with beauty and pleasure and love.

Some have a hard time imagining that Jesus, God's perfect Son, could have a desire that was in conflict with His Father, but we know of at least one time when He did.

46

Late one night after celebrating the Passover dinner with His best friends, Jesus took them to the place they often stayed—an olive garden across the Kidron Valley from the Temple. As they settled down for the night, Jesus asked His friends to stay awake and pray. This was no ordinary prayer request, for this was no ordinary night.

The drama in the olive garden was all about desire—the desires of the Father and the Son were in conflict. Jesus did not *want* to die. He did not *want* to bear the weight of the world's sin. He pleaded, "My Father, if it is possible, may this cup be taken from me." But He *wanted* to do the will of His Father. He *wanted* to fulfill the purpose for His life on earth. So He added, "Yet not as I will, but as you will" (Matthew 26:39). God, on the other hand, wanted to complete His plan of salvation, and the success or failure of His plan depended on the desires of His Son.

Jesus wanted God's will more than He wanted to save His own life. He wanted to fulfill God's purpose more than He wanted to feel pleasure or avoid pain.

In the beginning, Eve got what she wanted, but not what we needed—knowledge of evil. In the end, Jesus got not what He wanted, but what we needed—innocence of evil.

Mel Gibson's movie *The Passion of the Christ* presents a gruesome and graphic picture of Christ's final hours on earth. The physical torture is unimaginable, the emotional torment incomprehensible. But for Jesus, the separation and alienation from His Father was worse than the beatings of the Romans or the betrayal of His friends. Who can imagine being separated from all that is good and beautiful? Who can imagine being in a place where God's grace and mercy don't exist?

The passionate arguments that swirled around

Gibson's movie boiled down to this: No one wants to be blamed for killing Jesus. Even those who don't believe that Jesus is God's Son or Israel's Messiah want nothing to do with His death. Many Christians tried to silence the critics by arguing that everyone is equally to blame, but that failed to satisfy those who want no part of it.

By allowing the focus to remain on *who* is to blame, we can miss the point of *why* Christ died, which was so that none of us would have to take the blame.

Christians fail to recognize the ongoing spiritual battle for their hearts, the place where God's glory is reflected.

VINCENTE BACOTE

Jesus came not as the Jews expected—in power and might to rule the earth; He came in weakness and humility to rule in human hearts—precisely the place where the perfect order of creation was first broken. Jesus came to claim worshipers who delight in Him. And He finds them not among people who deny their guilt but among those who believe in the power of His resurrection.

The Power of Resurrection

Both of my grandfathers were gardeners. They delighted in the beauty of flowers. Even though they've both been dead for many years, I never plant flowers or walk through a garden without thinking of them. And I never see daffodils in the spring without thinking of my grandmother.

The last words I heard her say were, "Walking through Daddy's flowers." She repeated this phrase again and again in a slurred, unfamiliar voice as my friend and I, both eleven, tried to get Grandma back into the house after finding her lying in a field of Grandpa's golden daffodils.

My grandfather had died the previous fall, but his

flowers, buried as they had been all winter in anticipation of spring's glorious resurrection, were still unaware that the one who planted them would not be around to welcome them when they poked their heads out of the ground. He was now anticipating an even more glorious resurrection—his own.

Perhaps Grandma was breaking the news to them about Grandpa when she suffered the stroke that would reunite her with Grandpa one week later. I will never know because she slipped into a coma before slipping off to meet Jesus and Grandpa. But I suspect that the bobbing yellow heads and the sweet scent of Grandpa's flowers made Grandma long for a better place.

What is it about a field of daffodils that causes emotions strong enough to carry my grandmother into the presence of her heavenly Father and her loving husband?

Beauty. What is it about smelling a rose that makes exhaling such an unwelcome necessity? *Beauty*. What is it about tasting a cold sweet beverage that makes us savor every sip? *Beauty*. What is it about hearing great hymns of faith that brings a lump to our throats? *Beauty*. What is it about touching the soft, smooth skin of a newborn that brings tears to our eyes? *Beauty*.

God, in His bountiful love, has created beauty for every one of our senses to enjoy.

Beauty makes us yearn for something more, makes us strive for something better, makes us believe in something perfect. Beauty is God's way of whetting our appetites for all that He wants to give us.

Few people deny the power of beauty, but many argue about whether it's a vice or a virtue. Is it a godly goal or a vain ambition? Is it a way to reveal God to others or an attempt to draw attention to ourselves? Is it a gift from God or the lure of His adversary?

Beauty, I believe, is all of the above. Beauty is a gift from God that sin has corrupted. Having nothing of his own to offer anyone, Satan takes what is good and uses it for evil. The reason we are so easily deceived is because Satan dresses evil in its Sunday best before introducing it to us, and our emotions run away with it before our brain has thought of any questions to ask.

One pastime I enjoy is reading gardening magazines in the bathtub. Although I love this relaxation, I eventually become restless. I am not satisfied to simply view beauty; I need to create my own. So I pull my shriveled body out of the bubbles, get into my gardening clothes, and head outdoors with trowels and pots of perennials.

As I do, I ponder the idea that going to church should

be the spiritual equivalent of reading gardening magazines in the bathtub. Church should be a place where the majesty of God is displayed in such a grand and glorious way that I can hardly wait for the service to end so I can go out into the world and plant a garden of spiritual beauty, which, like Grandpa's garden, will make all who experience it long for a better place.

The Power of Beauty

Beauty has been the primary factor in convincing me that God is not only great (i.e., strong) but also good (i.e., loving). The beauty of music and the ability God gives to humans to create it leaves me in awe. Singing in choirs has helped me realize that Christianity is more than mental assent to a set of beliefs, and more than agonizing self-discipline to get my body to obey a set of rules. The beauty of music lifts me to a new level of understanding; I can actually enjoy living for Jesus because Jesus wants nothing but good for all creation, including me.

As I sing, my belief in God becomes more than a mental exercise; it becomes a thing of beauty that stirs passion and a desire for goodness in my soul. Our choir director's ability to pull beautiful music out of mediocre musicians became for me a metaphor of what God was doing in my life and in the world. I wanted to be on God's side not just because He is strong and scary, but because He is loving and good.

Although truth is certainly important to God, He doesn't expect it to stand alone. God adorns truth with beauty and goodness, making it into something that appeals to every aspect of our being—our hearts and souls and bodies as well as our minds.

This realization came to me unexpectedly one Easter morning. The church was filled with worshipers, and two hundred choir members dressed in white robes filled the loft and lined the aisles for the closing song—a medley of hymns ending with "Crown Him Lord of All" as banners bearing the names of God were carried to the front of the church. A spotlight highlighted each banner as it moved slowly and majestically forward. Then came the final banner. As the choir reached the triumphant ending of the song, the banner reached the front of the aisle, and the people in the pews could read what it said: *Jesus.* In one unplanned, unrehearsed expression of unity, the entire congregation rose as if they were one person and stood as the choir sang the triumphant ending and then began to softly sing "Holy, holy, hallelujah, the Lamb has overcome."

People all around me had red eyes and wet cheeks, and my own heart was so full of emotion that suddenly even singing wasn't enough to express all that was happening in my heart. The tears collecting in my eyes were like water from a melting glacier, a glacier made up of all the ice-cold facts about God that I had stored in my head over the years. But that morning, the warm light of Jesus shone on my cold, rigid cache of knowledge and turned it into a torrent of emotion that poured into my heart and soul. At that moment I couldn't imagine why anyone would reject Christ. Nor could I imagine how heaven could be any better than what I was experiencing right then, right here on earth.

The beauty of the music, the passion in our singing, and the choir director's constant admonition to "sing for Jesus" made me want to renounce the sin in my life and do whatever I could to bring the beauty of Jesus to the world around me.

How does God love us with all His heart? By placing us in a world filled with beauty and pleasure—all waiting for us to enjoy at no cost. How do I love God with all my heart? By letting Him soften my heart until it overflows in praise and generosity and kindness and goodness and gratitude.

Around the world, Jews still celebrate Passover in much the same way Jesus and the disciples did in the upper room two thousand years ago. In doing so, they are obeying God's command to remember His supernatural work through Moses in delivering them from slavery in Egypt. The symbol of their deliverance was the blood of the Passover lamb.

It is no coincidence that the last meal Jesus had with

His disciples was the Passover dinner. He told them that this Passover celebration was different. He said, in fact, that it would be the last Passover meal they would eat together. Jesus even said that He would soon become their Passover meal. But they couldn't comprehend what in the world He was telling them.

When the meal ended, the disciples were sleepy from all the wine and food they had consumed. Eager to find a place to settle down for the night, they left the upper room and headed east across the Kidron Valley to a familiar hillside, the Mount of Olives, where they often spent the night.

In the olive garden at the foot of the mountain, the weary disciples, minus the one betrayer, settled among the rocks and tried to make themselves comfortable. But for Jesus, the time for comfort had passed.

That night as the city across the valley finished celebrating the Jewish holy day, Jesus began to feel the weight of the responsibility He was about to bear. His disciples, however, felt only the weight of their own heavy eyelids, and they were soon asleep.

On that night more than any other, Jesus needed someone to understand His distress, to pray with Him for God's intervention, to join Him in His suffering. But instead of having those needs met, He began to experience the terror of being alone—totally alone.

In the garden where Jesus prayed, olives were not only grown but also crushed and pressed. The crushing released the oil from the fruit, and the pressing separated the oil from the mashed fruit and pits making the oil suitable for use.

There beside the olive press, Jesus began to feel the

crushing weight of the world's sin coming down on Him. And there beside the oil press, He began to spill His lifeblood for the world's redemption.

Each of us has felt the crushing weight of sin. Some are feeling it even now. Sometimes it is the weight of our own sin and the shame and embarrassment of having failed miserably. Sometimes we battle temptations that feel irresistible. Sometimes we even get trapped in adultery, addiction, or abuse.

At other times it is the load of someone else's sin that weighs us down—someone who betrayed us, deceived us, abandoned us, ridiculed us, cheated us, or made a fool of us. Perhaps it is an unfaithful spouse, a wayward child, or an abusive or alcoholic parent. Sometimes it is another Christian who treats us unjustly.

Think about a time when the weight of that sorrow

was so heavy that you couldn't pull yourself out of bed.
Now try to imagine the heaviness of the combined grief
and pain of everyone in your family, your church, your
neighborhood. Add to that all the suffering that sin has
caused everyone in your city, state, nation, and the world.
Now try to imagine the accumulated grief sin has caused
throughout the centuries since creation. Just for a minute,
try to imagine . . .

Is it any wonder that the pressure of it began
squeezing the life out of Jesus on the night when God
began placing the weight of it on Him?

Just as millstones separate the oil from the flesh of the
olive by crushing the fruit, the weight of sin crushed
Christ and separated His blood from His flesh. All that is
true, good, and beautiful lay rejected, deserted, and
hideously disfigured in a cold dark cave.

Sin put God to the ultimate test. But His love endured it, His strength bore it, and His power overcame it. That is why we know beyond any doubt that sin—ours or anyone else's—will not and cannot win.

In Hebrew, *Hallel* means "praise." In celebrating Passover, the Jews sing "Hallel" (Psalms 113–118) both to please God and also for their own pleasure. The Passover ceremony builds to a great crescendo of appreciation for freedom and the beauty of life, and it ends in such a high emotional state that participants *want* to sing and praise God.

Near the end of the Passover meal, after the third cup of wine, the second half of the Hallel psalms are sung. The gospels say, "When they had sung a hymn, they went out to the Mount of Olives" (Mark 14:26). Imagine Jesus, on the night He was betrayed, on the eve of His crucifixion, singing a hymn with these words:

The stone the builders rejected

has become the capstone;

the LORD has done this,

and it is marvelous in our eyes.

This is the day the LORD has made;

let us rejoice and be glad in it.

Psalm 118:22–24

Loving God with all my heart means having every desire satisfied by Jesus. It means having a heart so full of gratitude for God's goodness and beauty and love that it overflows in praise even on the darkest days.